CASTE

Table of Contents

Introduction

Every day, multiple news outlets - each with their own biases - expose various human biases in the world around us. Some of the biases have been repeatedly exposed, often inciting outrage, only for things to change very little or not at all. Other biases are so culturally ingrained that it is difficult to see them in the world objectively. For example, US President Theodore Roosevelt was considered by many at the turn of the 20th century to be quite progressive because he invited African American leader Booker T. Washington to dinner at the White House. He was considered very progressive for his time, yet his views on race are not acceptable by our metrics today. That is because public opinions on race have changed over the last 100 years, although they still have a long way to go. In 100 years, people will look back at how women are treated today and be just as shocked and appalled by the views that are considered progressive today.

Talking about biases is uncomfortable for us because it is painful to consider the probability that we might harbor irrational biases of our own, that we might be harming people with our biased opinions, and that we might be wrong. It is easier to perceive biases in others than it is to perceive biases in ourselves. Therefore, this book will not be a preachy, self-righteous book about how terrible we all are. Instead, this book will be a historical look at biases in others who have gone before us. If this historical approach helps readers recognize and acknowledge some previously unrecognized biases deep inside the recesses of their own hearts and minds, that is the beginning of a good thing.

Chapter 1

Racism

Racism is a phenomenon that periodically grabs the public's attention, then seems to disappear from view. Racism persists because it should not persist – we know that discriminating against an entire race is wrong – yet we also know that it is far more entrenched than most people are willing to admit. We want the acknowledgment alone to make racism disappear. Unfortunately, every nation has its history of racism, and in most cases, it is so ingrained that merely knowing that it is wrong is not enough to end it.

Acknowledging societal racism is one thing, but acknowledging personal racism is even more difficult. Race is one of the most easily recognizable features of a person. It is natural to start to assess a person when we meet them, even before we begin to talk with them. Those initial assessments are based first on our own experiences. When we do not have any experience with a particular race or very little interaction, we judge the person based on what we have heard about the easily identifiable group the person belongs to. From an evolutionary perspective, this is beneficial. The problem occurs when those initial assessments incorporate negative biases based on systemic racism. One of the most prominent examples of this is in the United States, where policies and laws were written to include slavery, which primarily targeted Africans and their descendants. Racism was institutionalized, so overcoming more than 400 years of history will require a constant look at why things were done a certain way before society can remove the institutional racism from the current systems. It will likely take decades, even if the focus remains on finding and undoing what has been a part of the country's culture for so long.

While the obvious racism issues in the United States are easily observable today, it is hardly the only one. The country is currently actively trying to work through the issues. Other countries have not yet recognized that there is a problem, so the systemic issues will remain in the foreseeable future.

Racism is a global issue, and every race is guilty of harboring racist ideologies against other races. It is such a prevalent issue across the globe that dictionaries have decided to change the definition to reflect the problem perpetuated by systemic racism more accurately. The first known use of the term racism in writing occurred in 1902, though it is possible that the term existed before this time. The existence of racism stretches back millennia, though, so we just did not have a word in English to express it before the 20th century. The following is the original definition in the Merriam-Webster Dictionary:

A belief that race is the primary determinant of human traits and capacities and that racial differences produce an inherent superiority of a particular race

This definition did not appear to be adequate by the early part of the 21st century, however. In June 2020, Merriam-Webster agreed to add another aspect of the definition that more closely encompassed the bias's problematic aspects. The following has been added to address how racism has continued to harm races within a country:

A doctrine or political program based on the assumption of racism and designed to execute its principles

A political or social system founded on racism

The definition will likely continue to evolve. The following are just a few examples of institutionalized racism over human history.

Some of the earliest recorded examples of racism appear as far back as Ancient Greece, and it was entrenched by the time the Roman Empire became the major European and North African power. Plays that remain from this time demonstrate the ingrained racial stereotypes of the period and racial hatred that was prevalent during the time. Discrimination was used to justify increasing the size of their empire, and turning the conquered people into slaves proved their (the Roman's) dominance. Many of the systemic problems based on racism throughout Europe and the places Europeans traveled later have their roots in this period of conquest. These practices were called "traditional" over time, justifying their perpetuation across thousands of years. Nor was racism the only type of bias that was institutionalized by this time, with religious discrimination becoming an increasingly greater problem under the Romans.

During the period of history known as the Age of Exploration (from the 15th century until the end of the 17th century), racism was often demonstrated against indigenous populations of the New World. During this time, genocide and slavery were two tactics used to remove native peoples from their lands. Both North and South America are frequently highlighted, but the problem occurred worldwide as nations, mainly European countries, sought to expand their wealth and power. Australia has a dwindling number of indigenous people because of the racist practices that saw the original inhabitants continually being pushed from their own lands. Even Canada has a well-documented history of ill-treatment of its indigenous people. This is a systemic example of racism that nearly extinguished entire races, and the problem has not been adequately addressed in any of the nations where this has occurred. There are still indigenous populations in all of the nations of the world who experience discrimination and are ignored by the systems into which they were forced. For example, native populations in North America are still forced to live on reservations where the land is often inhospitable. Illness and poverty are rampant on reservations, and to improve their lives they are often forced to leave their homes and try to integrate into the populations that once drove their peoples from their lands. The lifestyles established for them more than 100 years ago has made it all but impossible for the natives to survive and live the way they had lived for more than a millennia before the Europeans arrived.

Racism in Asia is all too similar to the racism that was spread during European exploration. However, the racism in this region is as much based on class and hierarchy, which often excluded outsiders. People of European and African descent were often treated as lesser because they were outside the established hierarchy.

There is often much crossover between racism and other types of bias, particularly xenophobia, which can make it more challenging to address a problem in some instances adequately. However, there have been some signs of improvement across the world, giving some hope that the removal of systemic racism will eventually be completed.

The abolition of slavery is perhaps one of the most notable instances of the removal of institutional racism, and that does not apply just to the United States. Slavery has been an integral part of the economy of many nations throughout human history. There are still some forms of slavery that are practiced today, but it is mostly along the lines of gender instead of race.

During the 1960s, the *Civil Rights Acts* helped end some of the most egregious and obvious forms of systemic racism, ending legislative acts like the Jim Crow laws, which created an inherent separation between white and black communities. Unfortunately, the end of Jim Crow laws did not go far enough as many cities saw minority populations being pushed to specific regions, ensuring that some form of segregation continued.

Both Canada and Australia have attempted to address the systemic racism against indigenous people through First Nations legislation. Canada passed C-86 in 2018 to provide more access to lands and financial resources to restore some of what was taken from the people who lived in Canada long before the Europeans arrived. Australia passed the *Environment Protection and Biodiversity Conservation Act 1999* to provide more support and protection to indigenous people.

Perhaps the most hopeful sign that there is a growing intolerance to blatant racism and systemic practices occurred during the Pandemic of 2020. Around the world, major and minor cities saw protests against these kinds of policies and police brutality. It is difficult to distinguish between these two problems because many police are required to enforce laws that are often based on racist systems. This is not a problem for just one nation, as the protests show. It is a problem that an increasing number of people feel needs to be addressed on a local and national level within their own communities.

Chapter 2

Classism

Classism is the discrimination of people based on their social class. While it is easy to think that this is not a significant problem today, it would be more appropriate to think of classism as social inequality to understand how far we are from resolving this issue.

There are typically four primary classes:

- Upper class, also called the owning class
- Middle class
- Working class
- The poor, which can overlap with the working class

One of the reasons this is often dismissed as a bias is because people tend to think of classes more in the classical terms: monarchy, nobility, working class, and peasants/serfs. Class structures vary all over the globe, but for thousands of years, monarchs were members of the highest class. Over the last 150 years, many parts of the world have thought they have largely eliminated these kinds of classes. In reality, the class structure has simply changed to reflect wealth instead of lineage. This creates the illusion that anyone can reach the upper class, but those at the top remain just as dedicated to ensuring that they retain their positions. With the current social inequality, it seems evident that the upper class has been very successful, as most people hold only a small percentage of the world's wealth. A very small percentage of the world's populations (less than 1%) own more than 40% of the world's wealth. This allows them to control far more of the direction of the world and prevent others from reaching the same heights. Classism is not gone; it has just shifted who is at the top of the pyramid. However, as the wealthy amass so much wealth that they cannot possibly spend all of it, capitalism is slowly shifting into a system that more closely resembles the older class structures.

The history of classism is at least as old as civilization, and there have been many diverse forms of classes across the globe. For example, most places around the world have had a separate class in the form of religious orders. Sometimes they are outside of the regular social order, like most places today. Other times, they have held more power than any monarch, as was the case of the Roman Catholic Church during the Middle Ages.

Two other considerations define a person's class: social status and cultural capital. Socialites and people with large networks fall into the first category, while clerics and academics/intellectuals fall into the second.

Classism refers to how to treat a person based on their social standing. Within the previous contexts, it is much easier to see how classism is still very much a problem around the world.

The history of classism is incredibly varied, primarily based on what societies consider to be important.

One of the most accessible, best-documented examples of classism is from Ancient Egypt. The social structure dictated who could interact with each other. There was also what we know now was the hazardous practice of marrying within the family, which resulted in some very unhealthy Pharaohs toward the end of several dynasties. Many of the native peoples in Central and South America, such as the Incas, Aztecs, and Mayans, had similar social structures, though they did not seem to have a similar problem with the severe results of inbreeding. Like the Egyptians, these civilizations included a class of slaves from territories that they conquered. Both the Ancient Greeks and Romans had slaves based on their own conquests. They made a new class based on inequality because of their superior military abilities. For most of the early days of civilization, strength was the primary means that put people at the top of the hierarchy. Over time, what was most important changed.

Perhaps one of the best-studied examples of classism was the Indian caste system. It dictated not only whom a person could marry, but with whom they could socialize. The Indian caste system was based on religion, specifically Hindu law. It had four primary categories:

- Brahmins – intellectuals and instructors
- Kshatriyas – rulers and warriors, who supported the Brahmins
- Vaishyas – traders or merchants
- Shudras – menial workers

Each of these four primary castes had its own subdivisions based on what roles the individuals filled. The upper classes lived in different areas than the lower ones, and had different facilities and wells, distinguishing them as being different. Another class included everyone else who was not a part of the caste system. These were the untouchables, and even the Shudras were above them. This class is where the term outcast (people outside of the caste system) originated. India was ruled by this caste system for centuries, creating inequality that lasted until roughly the 18th century by which time the distinctions had lost a lot of their importance. By that time, people were better able to move within the caste system, which was not possible during the earlier centuries.

While there are still problems with classism, it is not nearly as severe a problem as it was throughout much of human history. In many locations around the world, there is an opportunity to improve an individual's situation. However, during the early part of the 21st century, this is becoming increasingly difficult as financial inequality hinders the mobility of the majority of the human population. People are more aware of the inequality today and are less accepting of it than in most other points in human history. It has become harder for some people to meet basic needs, but there is a growing movement against the severe financial gap between the wealthiest and the poorest people. The last time there was such a significant difference, there were rebellions, such as the French Revolution. It does appear that people are beginning to advocate for change before there are too few options. With movements such as Occupy Wall Street, people seem to be seeking change through peaceful and more permanent means. Like racism, people have to work against classism continually. Unlike racism, people are far more aware of the social divides that do harm to the majority of people. There is an increasing awareness of this particular bias that gives hope that the constructs and hierarchies will eventually not create inequality, as they have throughout most of human history.

Chapter 3

Ageism

Ageism is discrimination or prejudice against a person because of their age. It is often considered the most egregious in its application against the elderly, but ageism applies to all ages. Young adults are often exploited by employers because they are young and do not know their legal rights. Middle-aged people may find it harder to get a job if they lose their old job. Older people are often at the greatest risk, however. They are more often pushed to the margins of society, with their health potentially suffering because of it. Police and investigators are less likely to examine the death of an elderly person because it is felt that they did not have much longer to live.

One of the most extreme examples of ageism is from the serial killer Harold Shipman. He was a well-known doctor in the UK during the latter half of the 20th century. It is unknown exactly when he first began killing his older patients, but he injected morphine into an estimated 215 patients before he was finally stopped. Since the vast majority of his victims were people in their 60s and older, red flags that were raised about how many of his patients died were often waved aside by police and people in authority because the patients were old. They were close to death, so their death was expected and not considered suspicious.

Unfortunately, this is not the only example of older people being a targeted group. Throughout history, many civilizations expected older people to sacrifice themselves in dire situations. Senicide is the long-established practice of sacrificing the old because their existence is seen as a burden since they cannot contribute as much as they require from the resources of a group. It has been practiced throughout nearly all of human history, including Native American, Eskimo, European, and Asian nations. The ideology is still a part of the way people think today. One of the most recent examples of this today occurred in the United States in 2020 when Dan Patrick, the Texas lieutenant governor, suggested that older Americans should be willing to risk death because of COVID-19 to save the United States economy. The argument is not new, and there is still a large swath of the population who do not necessarily agree, but they do not tend to be as openly opposed to it as they are to other forms of bias. People see a kind of logic to this, even if they have a hard time admitting it.

It is perhaps ironic that ageism is a problem because it is the only social identifier that most people will eventually go through as they age. Despite this, people tend to forget what the previous stages of life were like, and they perpetuate the same problems they faced at earlier ages. It is a cycle that is difficult to break because it has been rationalized for most of human history. When people were far less advanced and resources harder to come by, it is possible that senicide was necessary because it was impossible to feed everyone. However, this is no longer the case. Humanity is no longer in a position where people have to be sacrificed so that others can survive. The problem is that it is an attitude that was necessary for survival, so the mentality is ingrained. Because of this, it will be much harder to overcome this particular bias. It is much harder to recognize and remove ideas that once had a survival component for the species.

Despite even recent examples of ageism, there is much hope for this bias changing as people are increasingly aware of ageism as a real phenomenon. The ideas expressed by Dan Patrick received significant backlash from many different age groups. This issue has received very little attention in the past, but a growing number of organizations are making recommendations and warning people of the long-standing problem with ageist practices. In particular, the medical community is sounding the alarm, with the World Health Organization and American Psychological Association putting out recommendations and ideas on how best to address the issue. An increasing number of laws have been passed around the world to fight ageism as well. Agediscrimination.info provides an extensive list of nations that have passed anti-ageism laws to prevent companies and governments from discriminating based solely on a person's age. More than 40 countries appear on the list, showing a growing awareness of how detrimental ageism can be. Most of the laws have been passed within the last 50 years, showing that there is a growing trend to protect people of all ages, something that is unexpected considering it is a problem that still has not been recognized by the broader population. Given how long this has been a problem, it is definitely a hopeful sign of what is to come and how people will begin to value all the different age groups for their ongoing contributions to society.

This is one of the biases where all citizens need to earnestly contend with their own beliefs. It is much harder to realize that we have an inherent bias as that bias does change over time as we age. Seeing it when we are young can help to change things so that we do not perpetuate the problem when we are older. After all, societies where elders are respected for their wisdom tend to be the most peaceful and stable.

Chapter 4

Homophobia

Before getting into this chapter, it is best to recognize that this is when people are most likely to close the book and refuse to pick it up again. This is a bias that is still widely accepted, and there are many reasons that people use to justify it. It is also a very human reaction to become defensive about our biases – that is an understandable reaction. This book is not meant to criticize. Nevertheless, this is a serious matter, and it should not be dismissed lightly.

The best way to understand homophobia is through the definition of the word. Like racism, it has changed to include more than just the base meaning of the words. It is not merely a fear of homosexuality. The following is how Merriam-Webster defines homophobia:

Irrational fear of, aversion to, or discrimination against homosexuality or homosexuals

The term itself is only a few decades old (it is thought the term was coined in the 1970s), and many civilizations throughout history have largely avoided directly addressing it. It can also be challenging to distinguish homosexuality from other members of the LGBT (lesbian, gay, bisexual, and transgender) community as they are often lumped together, and they often do not make a distinction when pushing for equal treatment. They make up a small fraction of the total world population, though exact numbers are unknown because of how risky or deadly it can be to admit to being a member of this community.

Homophobia is a bias that recently has undergone some strong opposition by a much greater percentage of the human population. It is also the only type of bias that has not been a universal problem. Unlike ageism, racism, and sexism, there have been periods in human history when homosexuality was encouraged. For example, some thought in Ancient Greece that it was desirable in order to create a bond among soldiers so they would fight more fiercely to protect each other. The practice of having a relationship between two men is thought to have been encouraged as there were other benefits, particularly between students and pupils.

However, some people say that same-sex relationships were not allowed once a man was able to grow his own beard (very little is recorded about same-sex relationships between women, something that has seemed to be more acceptable in general over much of human history). According to some historians, homosexual relationships were strictly prohibited in Sparta, while other historians contend that homosexuality was encouraged among the troops. Sparta was a highly classist and militarily driven society where nearly every aspect of a person's life was dictated based on gender and class. It is hard to say whether Sparta actually encouraged homosexuality among the troops or not because it was not documented.

Homophobia is an incredibly complicated bias because it has many different forms and justifications. Some people view it as wrong based on their religion, which means that homophobia is a part of religious intolerance. Other times, people justify their bias because they see homosexuality as unnatural because it does not result in a child. However, there are many examples of non-human animals engaging in homosexuality, sometimes as a way to display dominance. Several species of birds have exhibited homosexuality, such as female albatrosses, where 31% of the female albatrosses on Oahu (a Hawaiian island) were a part of a same-sex couple. An estimated 20% of swans are a part of a same-sex couple, and they are known for mating for life. Nor have researchers found it being exclusive to birds or humans, with giraffes, dolphins, lions, macaques, and bonobos all engaging in homosexuality.

Whatever the basis for the bias, it has had some horrific results around the world for millennia. It is one of the only biases where one probably will not know that someone is gay or bisexual unless one asks or sees them with their significant other. Because of this, many homosexuals have been silent on their sexuality as it allows them to be treated like everyone else.

Many countries have laws against homosexuality, with the most severe penalty currently being enforced being death. In many other countries, there are few to no laws protecting the members of the homosexual community. This has been changing over the last 20 years, but there is still a long way to go.

This is also the bias where it is not necessary to go very far back to see some of the atrocities enacted against homosexuals. Trying to identify examples of historical homophobia is difficult because it was not directly recognized until more recently, although hate crimes against homosexuals have occurred over the millennia.

Oscar Wilde was a very popular Irish poet and playwright, who was accused and convicted of indecency with men (the British term referring to homosexuality during the Victorian Era). He spent two years in prison and was bankrupted because of his time incarcerated. He only completed one major work after he left jail in 1897. He died in 1900 at the age of 46. His last major work seemed to express his concern over the inhumane treatment of prisoners.

In New York City during 1969, laws dictated what people could wear to make it easier to arrest homosexuals. Any man who wore women's clothing (commonly referred to today as dressing in drag) and any woman who did not have at least three pieces of "feminine clothing" could be arrested. Cops knew which bars were more likely to be frequented by homosexuals, and they raided those bars regularly. On June 28, 1969, patrons at the Stonewall Inn bar decided that they were not simply going to comply with this discrimination any longer. When the police entered the bar, instead of lining up outside as they usually did, the patrons decided to fight the police. The event has been characterized as a riot, and the term "gay power" began to be used as the LGBTQ community began to fight against the systemic discriminatory behavior by police. The community initially reacted similarly to the Black Power movement that was also fighting police discrimination at the time. Over time, as activists took more peaceful approaches through sit-ins and protests, the term changed to gay pride. The events in New York during 1969 were the basis for today's Pride Month.

More recently, two serial killers were able to continue with their murders because of systemic discrimination against the gay community. In the US, one of Jeffry Dahmer's victims was only 14 years old, yet he managed to escape after Dahmer had left his home. Some women in the neighborhood found the boy naked and bleeding after his escape, and they tried to comfort him while calling 911. The police and Dahmer arrived at nearly the same time. The victim had been drugged, so he could not contradict Dahmer when Dahmer explained to the police that the victim was his 19-year-old boyfriend, and they had just had a fight. Instead of investigating, the police did not want to get involved with something involving homosexuals. They allowed Dahmer to take his victim back home without any real investigation. Had they gone into the apartment or looked into Dahmer's background, they would have known he was lying. At the time, the corpse of his last victim was still in Dahmer's apartment, and he was a registered sex offender, having molested his victim's brother several years prior and served jail time for it. Instead, they let Dahmer take the child back to his apartment, even though the two women who called the cops protested against it. The child was likely killed within a few hours of being returned to the apartment that he had escaped from on May 27, 1991. A few months later, some of his remains were found when Dahmer was apprehended on July 22, 1991, after another of his victims managed to escape and was more coherent when the police arrived.

In the UK, Stephen Port killed his first victim around June 19, 2014, after drugging his victim's drink and then used other drugs to cause an overdose. He left his victim's body outside of his apartment building and called the police to say he found the young man outside of his home.

Even though the police quickly found that Port knew the victim, because it became evident that they had a sexual relationship, the police accepted Port's excuse that he found the young man dead in his home after an overdose and panicked. Port killed three more men in precisely the same way, leaving their bodies in a nearby cemetery. When a woman found his second victim in the cemetery while walking her dog, she reported it, saying that it looked staged. When she encountered his third victim in the same location in the same staged position, the police accepted the "suicide letter" with the body saying that he was the lover of the previous victim, and he could not continue living after causing his "lover's" death. Even though the letter also explicitly mentioned that they were not to look into the man he was with the previous night because he was not a part of this - something that was clearly a red flag – the police again accepted this explanation and closed the case. It was only after the fourth victim's family refused to accept that their son, someone who was extremely opposed to drugs, had overdosed and essentially forced the police to release footage showing the man with their son the night that he died that the police finally started to follow their standard procedure. Again, their bias against the gay community made it possible for Port to kill three more times. After the first killing, a routine investigation would have made it evident that it was not an accidental overdose as Port's search history showed precisely what he had planned.

According to crime statistics, there were 7,120 hate crimes in the US during 2018, and about 19% of those hate crimes (over 1,300) were based on anti-LGBTQ discrimination. Based on the 2017 Gallup poll, less than 5% of Americans identify themselves as part of the LGBTQ community. The rise of populism in Europe has increased the number of hate speeches against the community, with more than a quarter of the LGBTQ community in Europe reporting either being attacked or threatened. According to the Trans Murder Monitoring Project, a member of the LGBTQ community was murdered every two days between 2008 and 2014. This number was based on murders over 62 countries and did not include violent attacks that did not result in death. It is unknown how many people identify within this community as it is unsafe in many countries to openly identify as being a homosexual or other member of the community.

There are arguments over whether a person's nature or nurture makes them a member, and we are not looking at that in this book. The problem is that there is currently such an intense hatred of those who are open about their sexuality that they are more likely to be targeted by hate crimes. LGBTQ people between the ages of 10 and 24 are five times more likely to attempt suicide than their heterosexual counterparts.

The primary problem is that it is more widely acceptable to hate this particular community than nearly any other bias around the world. This leads to violence and killings at a disproportionate rate, both by police and citizens. Whether or not one feels that being homosexual is right or wrong, it is difficult to argue that violence or murder is a justified response to it.

Homosexuality is something that has only more recently been identified as an issue that should be addressed. It was only during the 20th century that this community really gained recognition and their own identity, despite homosexuality being something that has been a part of human history. There have been many homosexual leaders throughout history, but generally, it is not certain who was or was not because it was either not acknowledged or they were not open about their sexuality. This is why people are identified as "the first openly gay" leader. It is almost certain that at least one (likely more) American President was a homosexual, but this was hidden from the public. Throughout history, people generally did not care as much about their leaders' sexual preferences. It is only more recently when the community has started refusing to try to act like everyone or to put up a façade of who they are.

It is challenging to say precisely how much progress has been made throughout human history. Homosexuals and others within the LGBTQ community have always experienced discrimination, but they were generally able to hide their sexual preferences. Today, we understand how detrimental that is to a person's psychological well-being, and the community is becoming more demanding about being allowed to be open about who they are without being afraid of being attacked.

Looking at crime statistics, it can be challenging to feel hopeful about the community's future, particularly as there are nations that explicitly discriminate against the community. The majority of nations with these laws are located in Africa, the Middle East, and western Asia, though there are several Caribbean nations (most notably Jamaica) where there are similar laws.

Despite the bleak statistics, there is a growing call among many nations for equality for the community. This is partly because the biases are more evident through cases like Dahmer and Port that show how the police have failed victims, and in part, because of video footage that shows exactly what the community endures on a regular basis. It has helped to turn opinion against discrimination because many people do not feel that violence and systemic bias are justified simply because they are homosexual. It has also started to make people question why they feel the way they do about the community. As more people come out as being homosexual, it is also becoming more evident that most people know at least one person who is in the community. In the past, many families disowned members who came out, but there is a growing acceptance because knowing that a person is a homosexual does not really change anything that one already knows about that person.

By 2020, there were 31 countries where same-sex marriage was legal, with The Netherlands being the first to pass such a law in 2000. Many other nations allow it in different regions, indicating that at some point, a final ruling will need to be made to allow it. In 2020, the US Supreme Court ruled that companies are not allowed to discriminate based on a person's sexual preference. The European Union banned similar discriminations back in 2000. In Australia, discrimination based on sexual orientation was banned in 2013 as an amendment to the *Human Rights and Equal Opportunity Commission Act of 1986*.

Chapter 5

Religious Intolerance

Religion has been a part of human civilization since before recorded history. It is often difficult to know a person's religion by just looking at them, although some religions make it easier to identify members by requiring certain practices or the wearing of specific clothing. The Encyclopedia of World Problems & Human Potential defines religious intolerance as follows:

Religious intolerance involves acts denying the right of people of another religious faith to practice and express their beliefs freely. Religious intolerance is expressed in discrimination, repression, and religious rivalry, and results in or result from persecution. It leads to war and persistent hatred between nations and between peoples within nations.

This definition is important because it shows how detrimental religious intolerance can be. Many of the most notable and infamous atrocities were committed in the name of religion, from before Biblical times through the modern-day. There were many examples in history when this bias resulted in significant amounts of bloodshed.

The *Bible* provides one of the earliest documented examples of religious persecution when the Jewish people were not allowed to hold certain positions of authority and were kept in a low social order under the Egyptians. According to the book of Exodus, Hebrews were slaves in Egypt. When the Egyptians thought that there were too many of them, the Egyptian pharaoh ordered that all male babies were to be killed after they were born. After baby Moses's mother placed him in a basket to save his life, he floated down the river until he reached the place where he was found by the Egyptian royal family, who then adopted him. Despite being raised by the most powerful family in Egypt, Moses went on to help the Hebrews leave Egypt. The *New Testament* of the *Bible* provides a look at religious intolerance that Christians face. Under the Roman Empire, Christians were brutally killed for sport because they followed a nonviolent policy. Christians were placed in arenas and were eaten by lions to entertain the audience.

The Crusades occurred over 1,000 years later and saw Christians marching into the regions that were sacred to their religion and had been taken over by the followers of Islam. The First Crusade had marginal success, but subsequent Crusades only resulted in perpetual bloodshed without any benefit to either the Christians or the followers of Islam. While attacking Muslims, Christians also slaughtered a large number of Jews simply because Christians still held a grudge because of the crucifixion of Jesus. Across much of Europe, there was much anti-Semitism during this time as well. The last Crusade ended up with the Roman Catholic Church's followers sacking Constantinople, the capital of the Byzantine Empire, whose citizens were Greek Orthodox Christians, the same people who had asked the Catholics to help with the First Crusade. Nor was this the only significant example of Christians killing each other over specifics on their religion.

The Protestant Reformation incited bloodshed between Roman Catholics and Protestants. There is no single war that best illustrates the religious intolerance of this time, but there was a steady series of wars between countries and regions that were firmly on one side or the other.

Perhaps the most famous example of this was when England's King Henry VIII broke away from the Roman Catholic Church so that he could divorce his wife and marry another woman. There is classism that allowed this to happen, but it divided England between people who wanted to remain Catholic and those who were dedicated to the king. This further division in religious ideology resulted in questions of succession in England after Henry VIII's son died far too young, and his Catholic daughter, Mary, became queen. She continued the killing, but this time it was the Protestants who were killed. When she died and Queen Elizabeth controlled the nation, more bloodshed followed as people were forced to follow English Protestantism instead of Catholicism.

A more recent and notorious example of religious intolerance occurred during the first half of the 20th century in what has come to be known as the Holocaust. The attempted genocide of Jewish people by the Nazis is one of the clearest examples of when religious intolerance goes too far. While Jews were not their only targets (Nazis also sent homosexuals, people of African descent, Soviets, Poles, and political dissidents to concentration camps), they made up a large percentage of the imprisoned population. They were also more frequently targeted for hate crimes in Germany. As a result of this religious persecution, an estimated 6 million Jewish people were killed. Unfortunately, the Nazis were not the only ones discriminating against Jewish people at this time. A ship with more than 900 Jewish refugees managed to board a ship and sought sanctuary in the US. They appealed to both the US and Canada, but religion played a significant role in having them turned away. They returned to Europe, where they disembarked in Belgium. More than 250 people were eventually captured and killed by the Nazis after they took control of the continent.

Current studies have found that religious conflicts were on the rise through 2019. Based on available FBI data, hate crimes based on religious conflicts in the US are the second primary reason for hate crimes, making up about 22% of recorded hate crimes. Unfortunately, in many places around the world, religious intolerance is getting worse and not better. In the early part of the 21st century, laws restricting religion were on the rise across the globe. An estimated 52 countries have strict religious regulations, including China and Russia. Even nations that have long claimed to be religiously tolerant have seen reversals on that tolerance, particularly in the US, the UK, and France. Religious intolerance is not a problem in just a few countries; it is a universal problem. Many nations have trouble separating church and state because faith is often one of the founding principles for nations.

In Nigeria, more than 12,000 Christians and Muslims have been killed over a decade in the perpetual war between the two religions. In the Middle East, Christians are often targeted for hate crimes, and their places of worship are regularly bombed. In the US and Europe, the roles have been reversed, and Muslims are often discriminated against.

The only religion that does not have an extensive history of religious oppression are the Buddhists, a religion that goes back about 2,500 years. One of the founding precepts is to be tolerant and accepting of other people and religions and to avoid persecution. This does not mean that there have not been examples when followers failed to follow Buddha's teachings, but it has made it more challenging to justify intolerance that is explicitly banned by the religion.

It is difficult to point to a single example of religious intolerance being ended, especially as there is no predictability in when or where it will rise up and be a problem. There is a growing number of people who are secular around the world. In part, the rise of secularism is because of how destructive religious wars have been. This is not necessarily a good thing, though, as it can result in people discriminating against all religions.

There are also many laws in place to prevent religious discrimination, but these are often overlooked by groups of people or governments attempt to undo those protections.

Ultimately, this is a type of bias that is best fought through being tolerant of people's ideologies. Most of us are already aware of this, but it can be harder to practice. This is one of the few biases that is entirely taught, and can be very difficult to overcome because it is ingrained into a society.

Chapter 6

Xenophobia

Xenophobia is often confused with racism, but the two are distinct - although there are some places where they overlap. There is also some overlap between xenophobia and religious intolerance and nativism. The following is Merriam-Webster's definition of xenophobia:

Fear and hatred of strangers or foreigners or of anything that is strange or foreign.

The more strict translation of the term based on its Greek origins is "stranger fearing." Today, it often translates to mistrust or hatred of people of a specific nation or nations. It is also a term that has more recently begun to be used to describe this particular bias. It started to be used around the end of the 19th century, a time when xenophobia was heightened around the world. Xenophobia did not begin then, it just took until the end of the 19th century for people to start to recognize that it existed, then started to understand how it was a problem.

One of the biggest problems with xenophobia is that it is often used by corrupt governments to create an artificial problem to gain more control over their people. By distracting people from real problems and giving their people a common enemy, the government appears to be the protector of the people. This does not mean that xenophobia does not exist outside of government interference, but it is most dangerous when used by governments. The worst examples of xenophobia are usually done in "ethnical cleanses." While there have been many examples of xenophobia throughout history, there is an alarming number of more recent examples that fall almost entirely into this category over the other types of bias.

The term ethnic cleansing was first used to describe the decline and dissolution of Yugoslavia and what happened to the people within the nation. It initially referred to the way the Serbians attacked Bosnian Muslims to remove them from Yugoslavia. This was not a genocide as the Serbians did not want to kill all of the Bosnian Muslims; they simply wanted all Bosnians to leave what the Serbians considered their lands. However, even if the complete annihilation of the people was not intended, it does not mean that slaughtering the Bosnians was acceptable. Eventually, Yugoslavia collapsed.

It can be argued that the Holocaust was as much an issue of xenophobia as it was religious intolerance. The Nazis did not care if people practiced Judaism or not; they wanted anyone of Jewish descent killed. Ironically, their leader, Adolf Hitler, seems to have had some Jewish heritage. Like the Holocaust, the Armenian genocide in the early part of the 20th century sought to commit genocide on Armenians in Turkey.

The Rwandan genocide is another more recent example of the worst that can happen because of xenophobia. Approximately 85% of the people of Rwanda were ethnically Hutus, but the minority group, called the Tutsis, had most of the power in the country. In 1959, the Hutus overthrew the minority control, and the Tutsis fled the country, with a majority of them going to Uganda. While in exile, the Tutsis created the Rwandan Patriotic Front, and they planned to retake control of the country. In 1990 they finally returned and started a war within Rwanda, a war that lasted until 1993. The next year, the President's plane was shot out of the sky, and the Hutus immediately blamed the Tutsis. This resulted in an ethnic cleansing. Tutsi women were enslaved, and men were killed. Extremists used propaganda to encourage the growing hate. For 100 days, the Hutus extremists slaughtered about 800,000 people, including moderate Hutus.

Not all xenophobia is so deadly, but it can continue to be insidious. During World War II, the US and Canada created concentration camps for people of Japanese descent. There was undoubtedly an element of racism in this move as the same action was not taken against people of German descent.

Xenophobia is a serious problem around the world today. The rise of populism, a current trend in most nations, puts the citizens' needs and interests over all others, typically when that is not necessary.

There are hopeful signs that xenophobia is being lessened, even as populism rises. Unlike much of the 20th century, there is a much more rapid backlash to the blatant xenophobia expressed by governments. While some people are buying into the populist-nationalist ideologies, there is a growing number of people who are resistant to the idea that foreigners or people of a specific nationality should be discriminated against simply based on where they were born. Globalization has also made it harder for xenophobia to gain traction. People can go online and actually talk to people from other groups and are increasingly less willing to accept the idea that people they have not even met are the enemy.

Chapter 7

Sexism

This chapter is one that many people will skip. Most of us are well aware of the problem, but it is easier to feel that things are "fair" enough because, in developed countries at least, women are no longer treated like property, and have largely been able to vote for more than a century. For many people, sexism is a bias that they do not even realize they have, in large part because of how indoctrinated we are about gender roles from the time we are born.

While the other types of bias have been prevalent throughout human history, it is difficult to argue that any are as ingrained or ignored as sexism. This is the type of bias that is most likely to elicit groans and eye rolls because we like to think that this is not a problem anymore. We know that both genders should be equal. However, we are equally aware of the statistics that prove that the two genders are not treated the same way. While females are disproportionately adversely affected by sexism, males have also been affected.

Merriam-Webster defines sexism as follows:

Prejudice or discrimination based on sex *especially*: discrimination against women

Behavior, conditions, or attitudes that foster stereotypes of social roles based on sex

The problem is not that we are naturally prejudiced against another gender, but that traditions were established millennia ago, and those traditions have been largely universal across most regions where humans live. When we first meet someone, gender is generally the first thing we notice, which is mainly a result of biology. We are taught to associate many stereotypes as we assess gender, though, and that is where the problem starts.

The hardest thing to do is to avoid getting defensive and dismissive about a bias. Women can be sexist against women; in fact, millennia of entrenched sexism has encouraged this kind of thinking.

When the United States founding fathers wrote the *Constitution*, they worried about indoctrinating slavery because many of the founders were aware that slavery was wrong. However, there is no record that any of them ever questioned why women were excluded from being able to vote. In England (and across most of Europe), women were not allowed to own anything. When their husbands died, they lost their homes because the sons inherited the houses. All around the world, women were either not allowed to have jobs or were incredibly limited in what jobs they could hold. During times of war, women have always been expected to step up to fill the jobs that men have traditionally held, and then are supposed to resume the "natural order" once the war ends. World War II is one of the most recent examples of women holding jobs outside of their homes. They were then quickly pushed back into their homes to take care of their families after the war.

There are still many nations where women are not allowed to vote; they are not allowed to drive or do anything without being accompanied by a male relative. Women are far less likely to be believed when they report assaults. Harvey Weinstein's activities against women were well-known in Hollywood. However, it took dozens of women coming forward to finally force the legal system to stop turning a blind eye to his activities. By comparison, it only took one male accusing Kevin Spacey of assault for there to be nearly immediate action; more people did come forward to accuse him later, but it only took one man to get the legal system moving.

Even when people believe a woman's report, the legal system is not consistent in how it sentences the criminal. Brock Turner was convicted of sexually assaulting a woman, and two men helped to capture him after seeing him committing the assault. Despite the conviction, a California judge only gave Turner six months in prison.

In North Korea, women are openly treated like second class citizens. In China, the One Child Policy has resulted in the abortion or killing of female fetuses and infants because males are thought to be more valuable. As a result, there is a disproportionate number of males to females in China, and the sex slave industry is currently a significant problem because women are being sold to men as brides against their will. Nor is China the only nation with a significant sex slave industry. Women and children are the primary victims of sex slavery, so women are disproportionately affected by this industry.

Perhaps more dangerous than the overt sexism is the way the world is often designed for males. Here are five statistics that show how considering only one gender harms the other, and how failing to address the problem simply pushes the resolution down the road.

- Car safety features are made for men, resulting in women being almost 50% more likely to sustain a more severe injury in an accident. The seats and belts are made for the typical size and weight of males, which means they provide less support and protection for women.

- An estimated 33,000 females under the age of 18 are married every year. Even more worrisome, many nations do not have any laws prohibiting the practice of child brides.
- Based on the current steps taken to close the pay gap between females and males, it will take more than a century before women are paid the same wages as men.

- There are only six nations (Belgium, Denmark, France, Latvia, Luxembourg, and Sweden) that offer the same legal rights to working women as men. On average, the other 181 countries studied showed women as having only ¾ of the rights as men.

- More than 1/3 of women in the world have been physically or sexually assaulted by their partners. In 2017, an estimated 87,000 women were intentionally killed, and 50,000 of those were killed by their partners or family members. That is an average of 137 women murdered every day by their families or former partners. Males who witness their mothers being assaulted by their fathers are more likely to do the same thing to their partners.

While this particular form of bias can feel overwhelming to fight because it is almost universal in how sexism is practiced (just to different degrees around the world), there are some promising signs for the future, largely coming out of the younger generations. The judge who sentenced Turner was ousted from his position the next year. When he was given a position as a coach to girls playing tennis at a high school, parents and students petitioned for his removal, and his employment was terminated. In 2017, the Women's March and the start of the Me Too Movement began to call into question the idea that women are treated equally in the US.

Conclusion

It is easy to look at the world and to feel that resolving all of the problems is hopeless. Sometimes it feels like things are progressing too slowly or that they are going backward. But we must not let that prevent us from trying to improve the world. The best way to make the world a better place is to better understand our own biases.

Being aware of the problems around us is incredibly helpful to all communities. It is easy to focus on the people who are harmed by these biases, but, ultimately, they do hurt everyone. By marginalizing one group, it creates inequality, and, over time, history has shown us how that usually ends. Wars, revolutions, and genocide are common resolutions to oppression, which is what these different types of biases create within communities and nations.

Over 35 truth commissions have been established around the world. These commissions are meant to investigate abuses around the world, including war crimes and human rights violations. Established within countries (currently in Asia, Africa, and Latin America), commissions are meant to hold repressive regimes, extremist organizations, and rebels accountable for their abuses. They look at abuses over periods of time instead of based only on a specific event that called attention to the problem. The bodies called together under the truth commissions are only temporary and result in a report that helps to document the root causes and escalation of the abuses in the relevant region.

While organizations and commissions can provide a more extensive method of fighting harmful biases, the most effective way of avoiding repeating the problems of the past is to be more aware of both our own biases, as well as the biases within our communities. Protests, vigils, sit-ins, and other forms of forcing change have repeatedly proven to be an effective way of combating problems. It can be exhausting, but we have seen progress for all of the biases surveyed in this book, and that is a reason for hope.

Made in the USA
Columbia, SC
02 October 2020

21817397R00036